101 Self Help Tips

Table of Contents

101 Tips to Find Motivation and Reach Your Goals 7

Chapter One – Tips for Finding Your Motivation....................................9

Tip *1 – Make a Deal with Yourself..10

Tip *2 – Leave Yourself Messages in the Morning.................................10

Tip *3 – Don't Hit the Snooze Button 10

Tip *4 – Practice Positive Self Talk..11

Tip *5 – Stay on a Regular Schedule..11

Tip *6 – Breakfast is Key 11

Tip *7 – Have a Morning Routine..12

Tip *8 – Participate in Morning Exercise 12

Tip *9 – Take One Step at a Time 12

Tip *10 – Keep Moving Forward 13

Tip *11 – Reward Yourself...13

Tip *12 – Leave Yourself Notes 13

Tip *13 – Track Your Progress 14

Tip *14 – Make Small Goals 14

Tip *15 – Work on One Project at a Time 14

Tip *16 – Turn to Others 15

Tip *17 – Clear Your Mind 15

Tip *18 – Think of Things the Energize You...15

Tip *19 – Listen to Upbeat Music...16

Tip *20 – Find Your Mantra...16

Chapter Two – Tips for Building Your Self-Discipline..........................17

Tip *21 – Plan a Routine..18

Tip *22 – Keep to Your Routine..18

Tip *23 – Have the Same Routine Daily 19

Tip *24 – Set Specific Goals..19

Tip *25 – Define Your Life to Fit Your Goals 19

Tip *26 – Organize Your Day..20

Tip *27 – Utilize a Pinup Board..20

Tip *28 – Talk Through Your Motions 20

Tip *29 – Celebrate Small Victories 21

Tip *30 – Compete with Yourself 21

Tip *31 – Challenge Yourself..21

Tip *32 – Allow Others to Challenge You..22

Tip *33 – Filter Your Mind of Negative Thoughts 22

Tip *34 – Talk Kindly to Yourself...22

Tip *35 – Develop a Can-Do Attitude...23

Tip *36 – Develop Positive Affirmations...23

Tip *37 – Break Your Bad Habits...23

Tip *38 – Make an Action Plan 24

Tip *39 – Have the Bigger Picture in Mind 24

Tip *40 – Focus on the Present 24

Tip *41 – Learn from Your Experiences...25

Chapter 3 – Tips for Managing Your Time 26

Tip *42 – Take a Step Back...27

Tip *43 – Have a Plan...27

Tip *44 – Stick to Your Plan...28

Tip *45 – Allow Time for Rest 28

Tip *46 – Prioritize 28

Tip *47 – Write Your Tasks Down..29

Tip *48 – Schedule Your Day 29

Tip *49 – Take Other Schedules into Account 29

Tip *50 - Plan for the Unexpected...30

Tip *51 – Carry a Schedule 30

Tip *52 – Decide What Results You Want to Attain 30

Tip *53 – Create Time Management Goals............................31

Tip *54 – Utilize Time Management Tools 31

Tip *55 – Learn to Say No 31

Tip *56 – Don't Multitask...32

Tip *57 – Be Organized 32

Tip *58 – Batch Related Tasks Together...............................32

Tip *59 – Eliminate the Non-Essential 32

Tip *60 – Leave a Buffer-Time Between Tasks......................................33

Chapter 4 – Tips to Change Your Thinking...34

Tip *61 – It's Not About You 35

Tip *62 – Don't Take Things Personally..35

Tip *63 – Try to Find the Good in Everything 35

Tip *64 – Collect References that Reinforce Your Positive Belief 35

Tip *65 – Practice Visualization 36

Tip *66 – Avoid Negative People 36

Tip *67 – Avoid Instant Gratification..36

Tip *68 – Live up to Your Values 36

Tip *69 – Stop Comparing Yourself with Others 37

Tip *70 – Look for the Good in Other People..37

Tip *71 – Practice Meditation...37

Tip *72 – Completely Focus on Present Activities...................................37

Tip *73 – Be Aware of Your Thoughts 38

Tip *74 – Minimize Activities That Stop You from Being Present 38

Tip *75 – Face Your Fears 38

Tip *76 – Have Faith in Yourself 38

Tip *77 – Trust in Your Own Value 39

Tip *78 – Be Optimistic 39

Tip *79 – Always Show Your Real Self 39

Tip *80 – Always Speak Your Mind...40

Chapter 5 – Tips for Reaching Your Goals 41

Tip *81 – Have an End Result in Mind..42

Tip *82 – Break Down Larger Goals into Smaller Parts 42

Tip *83 – Set Reasonable Time Frames..42

Tip *84 – Stack Your Goals 42

Tip *85 – Move on to New Goals When You've Achieved Your Other Goal 43

Tip *86 – Have Benchmarks...43

Tip *87 – Start with the Basics..43

Tip *88 – Start on Small Goals 44

Tip *89 – Prioritize Your Goals 44

Tip *90 – Don't Take on Too Much at Once...44

Tip *91 – Have Someone to Keep You Accountable..............................44

Tip *92 – Don't Become Discouraged by Obstacles 45

Tip *93 – Look for People Who Share Similar Goals 45

Tip *94 – Use Your Family and Friends as Sounding Boards 45

Tip *95 – Learn to Let Go of Negative Forces...46

Tip *96 – Talk to Your Support Group Regularly....................................46

Tip *97 – Listen to Advice...46

Tip *98 – Be Open to Change...46

Tip *99 – Set Your Sights High..47

Tip *100 – Think Beyond the Present 47

Tip *101 – Don't Settle When More Can be Done..................................47

101 Tips to Find Motivation and Reach Your Goals

Setting goals and achieving them is something everyone can do to improve their lives. While we all have goals that we want to achieve, doing so, however, can be difficult. Nearly everyone struggles to convert their goals into reality.

We procrastinate and lose motivation, and ultimately falter in the execution of our plans, leading us to become frustrated and defeated. This failure to achieve our goals, eventually causes us to lose faith in our abilities to move forward, leaving us feeling powerless to break out of old habits and improve our lives.

Setting goals can be a powerful tool that keeps us focused and sharp. They can be visual and mental reminders that we need to get things done. If we fail to create goals for ourselves, then we can also fail to succeed in whatever we choose to achieve.

Having a tangible set of goals that are written down and checked off when completed, can provide an amazing boost to one's selfconfidence, which can, in turn, spur us on to achieve further goals. This will then increase our chances of bettering our lives

and attaining a life-changing goal that we thought beyond our reach.

Fortunately, achieving goals is a skill that can be taught and learned. From being more organized to changing your mindset, there are numerous ways you can put yourself in a better position to conquer your goals. The following guide will provide you with 101 tips for finding your motivation, building self-discipline, managing your time, changing your mindset so you can finally achieve your goals.

Chapter One – Tips for Finding Your

Motivation

If you find that you can't bring yourself to go through the necessary actions to reach your goals, then you more than likely lack the motivation. Motivation isn't something that is simply found; you have to make it happen. If you find yourself in a rut, here are some practical ways to drive yourself forward to accomplish your goals and change your life.

Tip *1 – Make a Deal with Yourself

If you want to overcome procrastination and start getting things done, you need to make a deal with yourself. This deal can be either big or small. For example, you can tell yourself, "When I'm done with these reports, I can take a walk in the park and enjoy some ice cream." Giving yourself something fun to do once you complete your task can keep you motivated to get things done.

Tip *2 – Leave Yourself Messages in the Morning

There may be mornings when you look in the mirror and don't like what you see. This can quickly kill any motivation you have and quickly ruin your day. To avoid this issue, find a message that will inspire you to be your best, even if you don't look or feel it. Using a dry erase marker, write the self-affirming message on your bathroom mirror. This will help build your self-image and help you start your day on a positive note.

Tip *3 – Don't Hit the Snooze Button

One phrase that can quickly zap your motivation, "Just five more minutes." When you hit your snooze button, you're starting your day off by procrastinating the inevitable task of getting up and

going. Having an extra five minutes in bed in the morning isn't going to do you any favors and will kill your motivation.

Tip *4 – Practice Positive Self Talk

If you have trouble getting out of bed in the morning, start practicing positive self-talk. When your alarm goes off in the morning, instead of grumbling and hitting the snooze button, tell yourself, "I can do this!" By affirming yourself in this way, it will make it easier for you to get out of bed and get going in the mornings.

Tip *5 – Stay on a Regular Schedule

Knowing what to expect can keep you motivated, which is why it's important to know your daily schedule and stick with it as much as you possibly can. While things do happen that can interrupt a schedule, knowing that you have one planned and in place can make it much easier to keep on track and still stay productive during the day.

Tip *6 – Breakfast is Key

Eating a healthy and balanced breakfast is the key to starting your day out right. Food is energy, so by eating in the morning and choosing the right types of foods, you will remain focused on your daily tasks and goals. Even when you feel pressed for time, have

a go-to meal that will give you the nutrition you need to start your day off right.

Tip *7 – Have a Morning Routine

Having a morning routine can help you gain motivation to propel you into the rest of your day. Knowing what to expect and knowing that once it's done what comes next will help you make it through your day. Changes in your routine can make it difficult to think clearly and have a productive day. However, doing the same general activities in the same order can help you get going.

Tip *8 – Participate in Morning Exercise

Take a morning walk or head to the gym first thing in the morning can increase your motivation for the rest of the day. Regular exercise can improve your blood flow and keep you from feeling sleepy or lethargic throughout your day. Even participating in a simple stretching routine in the morning can help to increase your blood flow and get you moving.

Tip *9 – Take One Step at a Time

Concentrate on one action at a time. If you think about everything you have to do, then your energy levels will feel even lower. Take your routine one step at a time and don't focus on what you have left to do. When you only focus on the immediate action, you won't mentally deplete what energy you have left.

Tip *10 – Keep Moving Forward

Once you get moving, keep moving. Energy isn't something that lives in a bottle and can be taken on a whim. Sometimes you have to force yourself to keep going. Maintaining your momentum increases the chances that you will continue to be productive and finish what you started out to accomplish in the first place. Don't fool yourself by telling yourself that you'll be able to do it later. This is nothing more than procrastinating and will ultimately leave a lot of unwanted tasks sitting on the back burner.

Tip *11 – Reward Yourself

When you are faced with a difficult task or situation, setting up a reward for when you complete it successfully can help you remain motivated. Rewarding yourself for completing difficult tasks can keep you motivated to keep going with the job and accomplish it in the time frame you've set.

Tip *12 – Leave Yourself Notes

Leaving yourself encouraging notes in places that you often look can make you feel better about yourself. Writing encouraging notes to yourself can help to remind you that you can do it and make it through whatever challenges that life throws in your direction.

Tip *13 – Track Your Progress

When your list of to-dos seems longer than what you have completed, take a moment and think of everything that you've accomplished during a certain period. While you may not be where you wanted to be at that moment, you need to remind yourself that you completed some of your tasks. Giving yourself that small pat on the back will help to keep you motivated and help you to continue with whatever tasks you still need to complete.

Tip *14 – Make Small Goals

It is extremely easy to feel overwhelmed when you set your standards and your goals too high. Setting small and attainable goals from the start will help you stay motivated when you reach them so that you can move on to the next step. When you set your goals too high, to begin with, you can become discouraged too easily and feel overwhelmed.

Tip *15 – Work on One Project at a Time

You may think that multitasking is a good idea until you realize you have unfinished projects on your list. Not only do you still have to complete each of the projects, but it makes you feel like you can't even achieve one. To keep your motivation, you need to focus completely on finishing one project at a time, seeing it through to the end before you begin the next one. Not only will this keep your motivation because you've achieved what you set out to do, but you will become more productive.

Tip *16 – Turn to Others

Those around you can be great resources when it comes to finding your motivation. Find some supportive friends and family who can help you achieve your overall goal and provide you with the motivation you need when the going gets tough.

Tip *17 – Clear Your Mind

When you start to feel completely overwhelmed, it's best to step away from the situation and take a deep breath. Allow your mind to relax and clear itself from the stress that it might be currently experiencing. Going into something with a clear mind will provide you with the fresh perspective that you need to help you stay motivated and productive.

Tip *18 – Think of Things the Energize You

If you lack energy, you can think about things that energize and motivate you to give you the necessary boost to get moving.

Using whatever the thought is that will drive you, allow it to replay through your mind over and over again as you pursue the not so pleasant tasks that you might be facing when you're less than motivated and lack energy.

Tip *19 – Listen to Upbeat Music

Music has the uncanny ability to dictate your moods. Upbeat and positive music can help you get going when you have low motivation. Try finding upbeat music that you like to listen to and play them when you lack energy and motivation and see if they won't have a positive effect on your motivation and energy.

Tip *20 – Find Your Mantra

A mantra doesn't have to be long; it just has to get you excited. When you lack energy and feel unmotivated, it's those few words that remind you what matters to you and get you to take action toward achieving the goals you've set for yourself.

Chapter Two – Tips for Building Your SelfDiscipline

People who are more self-disciplined tend to be more successful in their lives and are better able to accomplish whatever they put their minds to. Sometimes it can be tough to keep yourself in line. Everyone has their temptations and vices that can cause them to stray from their ultimate goals.

However, having self-discipline will help you to define your limits and know when you're getting off track with your goals and expectations. So, if you find that you have no self-discipline, you

need to try and find ways to build that discipline and keep it strong whenever you see an opportunity to stray.

Tip *21 – Plan a Routine

Developing a plan and sticking with it is a great way to keep yourself disciplined. Taking the time to have a set routine and sticking with it on a regular basis can help keep you in line and keep yourself motivated throughout the day. It will take some time to get a productive routine down, but once you have it, it's a quick way for you to ensure that you are disciplined and able to stay motivated throughout the day.

Tip *22 – Keep to Your Routine

Unfortunately, life has a way of interrupting our plans, no matter how prepared we think we are. However, it's how you handle these distractions that will ensure you find success.

So, when you see that something is interrupting your routine, work on getting past it as soon as possible, so you can get back to your routine and carry on as if the interruption never happened.

When you can stick with your routine, you are more likely to keep the momentum of your day in high gear.

Tip *23 – Have the Same Routine Daily

It can be incredibly confusing if you change your routine too often. Have one routine and work towards keeping it consistent from day to day. A routine can help you continue a steady flow throughout your day. It might take a bit to get your routine in place, but once you do, you will get the driving force that will help propel you through your day.

Tip *24 – Set Specific Goals

Goals are an important part of your motivation. If you don't know what you're aiming for, then you'll do nothing but walk around in circles. Having specific goals in place before you go for it will help you find your motivation so that you can reach those goals. By knowing what you want and what you can gain from the activity will give you the motivation to give it your all.

Tip *25 – Define Your Life to Fit Your Goals

Knowing what you want to accomplish is a good factor to motivate you to succeed in achieving it. Once you know exactly what you want and what goals you need to set out to achieve it, carefully structure your activities around those goals. This can be simply telling yourself that you want to be at this place at this specific time.

Tip *26 – Organize Your Day

Take a few minutes in the morning to organize your day. Organizing your day can help you stay productive and motivated throughout the day. There is nothing more discouraging than not being able to find what you need and having to waste valuable time looking for it. Taking a few minutes to plan ahead and organize how you want to spend your day can help to keep you on track.

Tip *27 – Utilize a Pinup Board

Hang a corkboard someplace where you'll see it daily and pin your goals to it. Looking at your goals on a regular basis can help to rekindle lost motivation and get you back on track to pursuing them. This is an inexpensive and quick way to visually motivate yourself and keep you working toward accomplishing your goals.

Tip *28 – Talk Through Your Motions

When you talk through what you're doing, you tend to pay better attention to what you're doing. This can save you a ton of time because you won't wander around aimlessly and forget what you wanted to do in the first place. When we are more aware of what we are doing, we tend to make each movement count.

Tip *29 – Celebrate Small Victories

When you don't want to get moving and feel lethargic, praising yourself for the small things that you've accomplished will help motivate you and keep you on the right path to reaching your goals. While it might seem silly, it really can be a great motivator, especially when you're lacking the energy and drive to get through the day.

Tip *30 – Compete with Yourself

Competing with yourself can help you to get moving faster. Competing against yourself to do better than you did the day before can make you want to step up your game and push yourself to do better than before. There are many different ways that you can compete with yourself, so you can become better and improve your motivational goals.

Tip *31 – Challenge Yourself

Find motivation and self-discipline by challenging yourself to complete new tasks on a daily basis. Challenging yourself daily to complete new, more difficult tasks, can keep you excited and make you want to continue trying and can help you improve your habits.

Tip *32 – Allow Others to Challenge You

Competition with others will fuel your desire to continue on the journey to reaching your goals. Use those around you to help you become more self-disciplined and help you find motivation and success. A little competition can go a long way in helping you go further and accomplish more than you would under your own power.

Tip *33 – Filter Your Mind of Negative Thoughts

Before you can set your goals and be motivated to discipline yourself, you need to start filtering the negative thoughts out of your mind. This will allow you to begin to focus on what matters. Unless you cleanse your mind of poisonous thoughts, you will find it impossible to think clearly and believe in yourself.

Tip *34 – Talk Kindly to Yourself

To rid yourself of the negative thoughts that you nurture, you have to pay attention to your self-talk. In order for you to be able to move forward and reach your goals, you have to build a positive mindset. A positive mindset starts with talking kindly to yourself. It takes a lot of courage to be kind to yourself, but it is necessary if you want to find yourself in a better place.

Tip *35 – Develop a Can-Do Attitude

To effectively push yourself forward and embrace challenges, you have to develop a can-do attitude. Doing this requires a commitment to yourself that you will do whatever it takes to become more disciplined and that you will strive for what matters most to you despite all odds.

Tip *36 – Develop Positive Affirmations

One way to ensure that you follow through with your goals is to turn them into affirmations and repeat them daily. When you repeatedly say something to yourself with deep conviction, you affirm in your mind and compel it to accept that suggestion and to work toward fulfilling it. As soon as your mind accepts the suggestion as the absolute truth, it will focus its energy on it and make you take meaningful action to reach your goal.

Tip *37 – Break Your Bad Habits

If you want to become more disciplined so you can achieve your goals and become more productive, you need to get rid of all the bad habits that keep you from being the best version of yourself. Your habits shape your life, so if you want to build a good, meaningful life and accomplish all your goals, you need to eliminate the bad habits that keep you from fulfilling your mission.

Tip *38 – Make an Action Plan

Without an action plan, you won't be able to move toward your goals efficiently. A plan of action will provide you with a step-bystep guideline for moving toward each of your goals. With an action plan in hand, you can complete necessary tasks every day that are needed to achieve your goals. Break your big goal, into smaller, more manageable steps and work on them daily.

Tip *39 – Have the Bigger Picture in Mind

If you have difficulty starting tasks or you lose your motivation, stop what you're doing and recall your end goal and think of the bigger picture. Recall why you're pursuing the particular goal and reiterate to yourself the importance of having self-discipline for achieving your goals.

Tip *40 – Focus on the Present

If you want to make continuous progress, it is important that you learn how to live in the present. Thinking too much about the future can overwhelm you, making it extremely tough to work on the current task effectively. Likewise, when you live in the past and continue to remember the setbacks you've experienced, you're unable to take the meaningful action you need to continue to move forward.

Tip *41 – Learn from Your Experiences

Every experience that you go through, be it good or bad, should be seen as a learning experience. If you make a mistake, don't regret the mistake and don't feel bad about making it. Instead, focus on what you can do to improve. Accept each challenge and obstacle happily and wholeheartedly to stop yourself from fearing setbacks.

Chapter 3 – Tips for Managing Your Time

Life is nothing more than one task to complete followed by another. Life is busy. However, how you deal with your business can make a world of difference when accomplishing what you hope to achieve and reaching your goals.

If you're tired of not having the time to accomplish your tasks, you're not alone. A lot of people suffer from the inability to manage their time so that they can be more effective and productive throughout the day. However, the difference between them and you are that they aren't trying to change their behavior.

With the right time management skills, there will always be time to do what you want and accomplish your goals.

Tip *42 – Take a Step Back

Many people tend to jump right into their day without thinking it through. They have a list of chores in their mind and are planning on when they can complete which chore. However, without fail, something gets forgotten.

To keep this from happening to you, take a deep breath when you first wake up and take a step back from your busy mind. Take the time to write down your tasks so you have an idea of how much time each one will take so you can more effectively plan how you will tackle the list.

Tip *43 – Have a Plan

One of the easiest and most effective ways to ensure your success is to have a plan for accomplishing your to-do list. This is the one step that often gets skipped. Take time to think about where your tasks fit into your day. By planning and breaking down larger tasks, you can accomplish the more important tasks before tackling those tasks that might not be essential.

Tip *44 – Stick to Your Plan

If you throw you plan out the window at the first opportunity, not only have you just wasted your time, but you run the risk of quickly veering off track. When you make a plan, stick to it as closely as you can. While things will happen to prevent your day from going exactly as you planned, you tried to make your plan work the way you intended it to. Learn to quickly deal with the other stuff that comes up and find your way back to your plan.

Tip *45 – Allow Time for Rest

If you're busy, rest might be a foreign concept. Too often, people will push aside their personal needs in order to accomplish what it is they set out to do. To keep your motivation and reach your goals, you need to make a point of taking a break during your day. Depending on your circumstances, this can mean treating yourself to lunch, having a coffee date with a friend, or finding some time to read a few chapters of your book. Make it a point to have some time to rest so that you don't burn out.

Tip *46 – Prioritize

Sometimes, it's just impossible to accomplish everything on your list in a given day. There will be those days where everything wrong will happen, eating up your time. When you plan out your day, make sure to plan to complete your most important tasks

first. Give yourself enough time to accomplish them. If you have time to work on other things after you've finished, that's great.

Tip *47 – Write Your Tasks Down

In order to properly plan your day, you need to know what you're going to need to do in that day. Take some time in the morning to write down your tasks. By seeing what you need to do, you'll be more likely to get it done. When we get busy, we tend to forget tasks that we needed to accomplish.

Tip *48 – Schedule Your Day

Take the list of things you want to accomplish and make a schedule. Consider how much time each task should take to complete. With this information in mind, aim to complete certain tasks at certain times during the day. While it might not always work out the way you plan, at least you have some structure to your day.

Tip *49 – Take Other Schedules into Account

If you don't live alone, you need to make sure that you're aware of the schedules of others in your household. If you have children, their extracurricular activities can impact your schedule. Make sure that you know what the other members of your household

are doing and when they are doing it, to save yourself frustration later.

Tip *50 - Plan for the Unexpected

You may have the best laid out plans, but it never fails that something will happen that ruins those plans. Make exceptions in your schedule for things that might come up that you hadn't planned for.

Tip *51 – Carry a Schedule

Carry a schedule and record all your thoughts, activities, and conversations for a week. Doing this will help you to understand better how much you can get done during the course of a day. You'll have the opportunity to see how much time is spent producing actual results and how much time is wasted on unproductive thoughts, actions, and conversations.

Tip *52 – Decide What Results You Want to Attain

Five minutes before you start a task, decide what results you want to attain. This will help you know what success looks like before you start. After completing each task, take five minutes to determine whether you achieved your desired results.

Tip *53 – Create Time Management Goals

Eliminate your personal time-wasters. The focus of time management isn't actually changing time but changing the behaviors that waste time. For one week, set a goal to not engage in your biggest time-wasting activity, and see how much time you can gain.

Tip *54 – Utilize Time Management Tools

Whether it's a software program, phone app, or Day-Timer, the first step to effectively managing your time is knowing where it's going and planning how you're going to spend your time in the future. Time management tools allow you to easily schedule events and set reminders, making your time management efforts easier.

Tip *55 – Learn to Say No

Making a lot of time commitments can teach you how to juggle various engagements and manage your time. However, it can easily be taken too far. At some point, you need to learn to decline new opportunities. You should only be taking on those commitments that you know you have time for and that you truly care about.

Tip *56 – Don't Multitask

Multitasking doesn't work. Rather than splitting your focus to accomplish numerous tasks, devote your entire focus to the task at hand. Find a quiet place to work and cut out all distractions. Concentrate on one task at a time, only moving on when you've accomplished the task.

Tip *57 – Be Organized

Being organized will save you a ton of time. Create a filing system for documents and make sure every item has a place to be stored. Unsubscribe from email lists that you don't want and streamline everything you can.

Tip *58 – Batch Related Tasks Together

Different tasks demand different kinds of thinking, so you should allow your mind to continue to flow with its current zone rather than unnecessarily switching to something that is going to require you to re-orient.

Tip *59 – Eliminate the Non-Essential

If you want to stay motivated and reach your goals, you need to identify the excess and remove it from your life. By removing the non-essential tasks and activities, you can become more and

more in touch with what is significant and what deserves your time.

Tip *60 – Leave a Buffer-Time Between Tasks

Allow yourself downtime between tasks to breathe and clear your mind. When you rush from task to task, it can be difficult to appreciate what you're doing and to stay focused and motivated.

Chapter 4 – Tips to Change Your Thinking

Negative thoughts, doubts, and fears are quite pervasive. We all have doubts and are afraid. However, if you want to live a worthwhile life, you have to get some degree of control over negative emotions and thoughts. These tips will help you create a positive atmosphere, even when facing difficult challenges. With the right mindset, you'll have the best shot at staying motivated and reaching your goals.

Tip *61 – It's Not About You

It is important to remember that 99 percent of the time, how people behave is not about you; it's about them. You will never truly change your mindset if you don't realize that the behaviors of others have nothing to do with you.

Tip *62 – Don't Take Things Personally

Don't take things that happen personally, because everyone has underlying issues that are not apparent on the surface. Stop making baseless conclusions based on a tiny amount of information that you have of others.

Tip *63 – Try to Find the Good in Everything

Life is too short to live in misery and blame everything else on your problems. Never blame, complain or take things personally. Instead, focus on the more important things in your life, those things that you are grateful for.

Tip *64 – Collect References that Reinforce Your

Positive Belief

Deliberately collecting references to reinforce your positive beliefs will help to weaken your limiting beliefs. Think about two or three positive beliefs that will benefit you the most and start to collect real-life evidence to support these selected beliefs.

Tip *65 – Practice Visualization

Visualization is an effective technique for changing your belief and reaching your goals. Your mind can't differentiate between something vividly imagined and real life. Using visualization can provide your subconscious mind with manufactured pieces of evidence that will reinforce positive thinking in your mind.

Tip *66 – Avoid Negative People

The people you surround yourself with have a tremendous impact on your mind. If you spend most of your time around negative people who always put you and your abilities down, you would never feel confident.

Tip *67 – Avoid Instant Gratification

Avoid seeking instant gratification. The good feelings you get are only temporary and will disappear quickly. Instead, you need to follow your heart's calling. Put your best effort into everything you do, and you will experience long-lasting, happiness and satisfaction.

Tip *68 – Live up to Your Values

This is one of the single biggest factors that determine your selfesteem. To raise and maintain high self-esteem and shift your

mindset, it is important to take action and move toward living up to

your values.

Tip *69 – Stop Comparing Yourself with Others

We are all unique, so stop comparing yourself with others.

Instead, you need to learn to accept yourself completely, then find

your purpose, your mission, and work on it with all your heart.

Tip *70 – Look for the Good in Other People

What you give out, you will receive back 100 fold. If you give out

love and care to others, you will get affection and support back. If

you give out anger and hatred, you will receive the same in return.

When you treat others well, you feel good in return.

Tip *71 – Practice Meditation

The best way to become more present in your daily life and

change your mindset is to practice regular meditation. Meditation

trains your mind to be in the present moment.

Tip *72 – Completely Focus on Present Activities

Learn to be more aware of the environment around you when

participating in your day to day activities. Really look at things, noticing small details like shape, colors, taste, weight, smell, etc. This will allow you to cultivate present moment awareness.

Tip *73 – Be Aware of Your Thoughts

Start paying attention to the thoughts that are going on in your brain. Don't judge. Don't label any thought as good or bad. Just observe them objectively. Stop taking ownership of your negative thoughts.

Tip *74 – Minimize Activities That Stop You from

Being Present

One of the best ways to be more present and change your mindset is to minimize activities that make your brain dull and unable to focus on the present. Some activities make you present, and some don't. If you aim to become more present so you can accomplish your goals, then you have to remove activities that aren't helping you accomplish those goals.

Tip *75 – Face Your Fears

When you expose yourself repeatedly to your fears, it can begin to lower their intensity. It can help to take the sting out and make it more manageable for you.

Tip *76 – Have Faith in Yourself

One of the core pillars of strength against fear is faith in yourself, your vision and your ability to succeed. Believe in yourself and

your vision and know that you have all the resources you need to become the person you want to be and reach your goals.

Tip *77 – Trust in Your Own Value

Don't let any compliments boost your ego or any criticisms shake your confidence. Always do your personal best at the moment and continually look for ways to improve next time.

Tip *78 – Be Optimistic

Nothing is certain in life. When you expect the worst, you tend to fear the unknown. Instead, realize that you've been given a choice to create the future you want. In life, you get what you expect, so try and find the good in every situation and the people around you.

Tip *79 – Always Show Your Real Self

Always show your true personality. Never be afraid to fully express your thoughts and feelings. Let the world know who you are and what you stand for, and you'll come across as a genuine, confident person who inspires people to break out of their own shells.

Tip *80 – Always Speak Your Mind

If you don't think that anybody understands you, then you need to speak up and be assertive. Let people know who you are and what you need. This is the only way they can clearly understand you.

Chapter 5 – Tips for Reaching Your Goals

Have you ever wondered how you could set attainable goals, so you can make your dreams happen? You're not the only one who has hopes and dreams, but your goals may be too lofty to happen.

The goals you currently have may be a great overall result of smaller goals that you've set for yourself, but as your goals currently sit, you are setting yourself up for frustration and failure. Here are the best ways that you can set attainable goals that will encourage you to work towards a greater end result.

Tip *81 – Have an End Result in Mind

Having a clear focus on where you want your efforts to end up is an important part of setting attainable goals. Having an ultimate goal will help you as you try to achieve the smaller goals you have made. Having a solid focus will help you achieve more.

Tip *82 – Break Down Larger Goals into Smaller Parts

Help yourself reach your end goal by breaking it down into smaller steps, rather than becoming stressed by trying to accomplish it all at once. When you take on too much at one time, you can become stressed, which might cause you to abandon your goal completely.

Tip *83 – Set Reasonable Time Frames

If you try to do something too slow or too quickly, it can throw you off focus. Give yourself an ample amount of time to complete each goal, to make sure that you get the results that you're aiming for. Be reasonable and set time frames on your goals and your achievements.

Tip *84 – Stack Your Goals

Working on your goals in a stacked method, allows you to work toward a new goal while finishing out the goal you were already

working on. This will help you to start the next step while finishing the previous step. This helps you keep the overall goal flowing.

Tip *85 – Move on to New Goals When You've

Achieved Your Other Goal

Often times, once you complete a goal that you have set out to achieve, you might feel like you're stuck in a rut. This can become frustrating because you feel like you're no longer moving forward. Don't let doubts hold you back. Begin to work on new goals as soon as you feel as though you have accomplished your previous goals.

Tip *86 – Have Benchmarks

Check in with yourself frequently. Creating a schedule to check on the progress of your goals will help you to understand better where you are and what you need to work on next. Set a regular time for you to check up on yourself and be honest about the progress you are making.

Tip *87 – Start with the Basics

Once you've set the goals that you'd like to pursue actively, you need to start at the beginning. Take the time to figure out where you need to begin and take the process in small steps.

Tip *88 – Start on Small Goals

When it comes to setting goals, you'll find that some of them will be larger than others. Identify the goals that you can handle on a smaller level and work up from there. After you've learned to put some goals into action, you will figure out how you can tackle the larger goals to make them a reality.

Tip *89 – Prioritize Your Goals

Some of the goals that you set will be more pertinent to the place you are in your life and your career. Try placing importance on certain goals and set some aside until you feel you are ready to give them your full attention.

Tip *90 – Don't Take on Too Much at Once

Often when you are busy, you tend to take on much more than what you can handle at once. The strain of taking on too much can cause you to become stressed and result in you losing focus on what is really important. Always be aware of what your limits are an act accordingly.

Tip *91 – Have Someone to Keep You Accountable

Another way to can continue to work toward your goals is by having someone who can help to keep you accountable. By having someone to ask you about your progress or about how you feel about the goal can help you keep your goals in the forefront of your mind, so you can continue to work toward reaching them.

Tip *92 – Don't Become Discouraged by Obstacles

Life is full of obstacles and challenges. If you allow these things to stand in your way, you will never succeed in reaching your goals. When you face challenges in life, you have to find a way to face them head on and make it through the fire and to the other side.

Tip *93 – Look for People Who Share Similar Goals

Even if you already belong to an existing support group, there is always an opportunity to add to it and make it more diverse. They don't have to be people you've known for a long time but can be people you've encountered throughout your life that can offer you solid advice to make your goal easier to accomplish.

Tip *94 – Use Your Family and Friends as Sounding Boards

Your family and friends are who know you best. They might be able to offer you advice that is extremely helpful and that you may never have thought about yourself. Their advice can help you to pursue your goals with more ease.

Tip *95 – Learn to Let Go of Negative Forces

There will always be at least one person who will do whatever they can to discourage you from your goals. Don't let these people have a part in your life or your goals. Let them go and remove the negativity from your life.

Tip *96 – Talk to Your Support Group Regularly

Having a support group will help you make sure that you can talk about your worries and frustrations and get the advice you need to continue on your journey to making your goals into realities.

Tip *97 – Listen to Advice

Take the advice that is worth listening to and make it a part of your goal. Don't think that you know everything. Allow yourself the vulnerability to know when you need to take advice or let the advice go.

Tip *98 – Be Open to Change

Change can be difficult for everyone. However, the more open to change that you are, the easier the transition will be when you are ready to make changes in your life. There will come a point in your life where things will need to change in order for you to be successful. Don't fight it, embrace it and continue moving forward.

Tip *99 – Set Your Sights High

It's okay to dream. You can get more done and be more successful when you take the time to set your goals and ambitions higher. Don't be afraid to set your dreams high.

Tip *100 – Think Beyond the Present

Having the ability to look past the present and set your sights on your future and your goals can make your current situation temporary. You can only go as far as you allow yourself to go.

Tip *101 – Don't Settle When More Can be Done

Settling when you know you can do better, only cheats you out of what greatness your life can really hold. You can realize more success when you push yourself further.

Everyone has big dreams, and we tend to make even bigger plans to fulfill them. Unfortunately, as time passes, we tend to lose motivation and enthusiasm in working toward reaching our goals, leaving us stuck in the same place, toiling away at our 9 to

5 jobs, trying to earn just enough money to survive.

Each of us has a positivity inside that serves as the source of our great ideas and accomplishments in the world. In exerting more effort in finding our motivation, we can achieve our ultimate goals and find the passion in our lives.

Utilize these 101 Self Help Tips to kick out the negativity and eliminate the stress that has been controlling your life. Don't wait, break the barriers that are keeping you from reaching your goals, break free from the cocoon, and finally win control over your life.

Printed in Great Britain
by Amazon